Tee-I

MW01028861

The FUNdamental guide for coaches and parents on coaching and understanding the sport of tee-ball (and the next level up) and having fun at the same time.

Douglas P. Kalbaugh

Douglas P. Kalbaugh

ISBN-13:978-1544806754
ISBN-10:1544806752
Library of Congress Control Number:
CreateSpace Independent Publishing Platform,
North Charleston, SC

DEDICATION

This guide is dedicated to my sons Nick & Austin, my two athletes. I have always loved coaching you both in baseball and soccer. You both have always made me extremely proud of your awesome efforts and great sportsmanship. You have grown into fine, young men and I am very proud of you both.

And to my identical twin brother, Darryl, for always being my Hero & my best friend. I have always looked up to you and admire your courage.

To my beautiful wife Carolyn for always loving me, taking care of me and encouraging me. You give me a great deal of strength.

And to my stepson Skye for putting up with me, growing closer to me, and for allowing me to be your second father.

My love and a heart full of gratitude to all 5 for their never-ending love and support!

Acknowledgements:

A huge thank you to Nicholas Kalbaugh for being our photographer and contributing the photos in this book. And also to Gabriel Garza for being a great baseball model for the photos.

Douglas P. Kalbaugh

CONTENTS

Table of Contents :

The Throw
Gripping the Baseball
Chose Your "Thunder-Stick"

Chapter Five : All About Batting
Up at Bat
The Stance
Knock-Knock Grip
Where Should The Back Elbow Be?
Load and Stride
Squash The Bug
Watch The Ball
Don't Throw the Bat!

Chapter Six : About the Bases
Foul & Fair
Base Running
No Blocking (Bases or Home Plate)
Using Base Coaches
Fielding Ground Balls
Base Coverages
Be Alert…Charge!

Chapter Seven : Where to Throw the Ball
Throw to First…
Throw to the Catcher…
When In Doubt…Throw the Ball to the Pitcher
Force Out Play
Double Play
Fly Out
Field Rotation
Good Sportsmanship

Tee-Ball 101

The FUNdamental guide for coaches and parents on coaching and understanding the sport of tee-ball (and the next level up) and having fun at the same time.

This "Tee-Ball 101, Coaching Beginning Baseball" guide is not only for coaches, but for parents as well. This guide will help you learn how to coach young athletes starting out in America's pastime game.
If your child is about to play tee-ball and you want to understand what that includes, or you want to Manage/Coach the team, you can gain a great deal of information from this book. After reading this guide you will feel more confident and prepared.

This guide will also cover information, such as specific techniques, that will help to prepare you for coaching the next division level up above tee-ball too. You can continue to build on this knowledge and instruction.

As a parent, having this information will keep you involved with your child during an exciting time in their life. He/She will always fondly remember these times with you as their coach or as their cheering section.
Let's get started and "Play Ball!"

Coach Doug Kalbaugh

Introduction :

So you've agreed to coach Tee-ball! (Or maybe you were roped into coaching the team because no else volunteered.) Well, first let me say, "Congratulations!" You had the courage to step up to the plate (pun intended), when others probably did not. If you are wondering, "What have I gotten myself into?!", do not worry. "You can do this"! Just remember the most important thing – It's all for the kids! The second most important thing to remember is, "*It's only a game!*"

I wrote this guide mainly to help 1st time Coaches/Team Managers, but it can also help those of you who have coached youth tee-ball baseball before. This guide will also cover information to prepare you for coaching the next division level above Tee-Ball.

Note: This guide applies to most tee-ball leagues, especially non-competitive leagues, but check the rules in your league for possible subtle differences.

I tried to cover many of the basic fundamentals of coaching beginning baseball and by having this guide you will not have to remember every little thing. You can just look it up in Tee-Ball 101. Stay positive and have a great season, Coach!

Divisions of play for beginning baseball:

The very first baseball division is Tee-ball, which goes into 'Coach Pitch'. This division is typically structured for children ages 4-6 and is considered an instructional division. Here coaches endeavor to teach the basics of baseball, good sportsmanship, and how to play together as a team unit to these beginning players. No scores or standings are kept in this division and there are no strikeouts.

The next baseball division after tee-ball is called 'Caps' (or something similar depending on your league). It is typically structured for children ages 6-8. The Caps division is also an instructional division, which endeavors to build upon the skills previously learned in Tee-ball & Coach Pitch. In this division the players hit a ball pitched to them by a pitching machine. The machine may be electric, (which automatically propels the baseball forward), or a spring-activated pitching stand. The coach first loads the ball onto the spring-activated pitching stand and then manually releases a lever to propel the ball forward to the batter. The pitching machine is utilized for more accurate pitches and gets the players ready to play in the next division up. If the players are unable to hit the machine pitched balls, they will be given the opportunity to hit from the batting tee. No official scores or standings are kept in this division either.

Even professionals use a batting tee!

Great job team!!

Reminder:

Take pictures during your season so you'll have memories to enjoy with your player later on.

CHAPTER ONE - All of the Basics
Getting Started

Let's get started. While managing a team and coaching tee-ball, you want the kids to have fun! Having fun is the main objective. Some will say, "Teaching the basics of baseball is the main objective". Obviously, we want to teach the players the *FUN*damentals of baseball, but the bottom line is, if they're not having fun they will not want to play at all, let alone, learn the basics.

Your main goals should be : 1. Teaching the Fundamentals of Baseball, 2. Player Safety, and 3. Sportsmanship. You want to do all of this in a way that will make the players return and want to play again next season!

The tee-ball players will probably range in ages from 4 to 7, so you will need plenty of patience and a good sense of humor. Obviously there will be varying degrees of ability on your team. Most of the players probably have never thrown a ball or even thought about catching one in a glove yet. Your others players have probably played last season and you may have some who are naturally inclined to be athletic. Talk about **Teamwork** with your team and have the more experienced and coordinated players help out the less experienced and less coordinated players during practices. To be successful, they all have to work together as a team, just like in the major leagues.

Once you have been assigned a team from your league representative, you will want to set up your first team meeting. The purpose of this meeting is to introduce yourself, meet your team and their parents, go over your own coaching philosophy, (if you have one, If not, you will soon develop one), go over the team rules, set a practice schedule and generally discuss the upcoming season.

Things to Cover at the First Team Meeting (There's a lot to cover here, Coach)

Welcome everyone and thank them for showing up at your first team meeting. Then introduce yourself and explain that this is your first year coaching tee-ball. If you have coached tee-ball before (or another sport, such as youth soccer), you can include this experience as well in your introduction.

Either way, the parents will be appreciative that you are doing this for their children. (Remember, they could have stepped up to coach, but they did not.)

Here is an example of my meeting agenda. You can type up a copy of it if you would like.

THINGS TO COVER AT 1st TEAM MEETING:

INTRODUCTION: My name is _____. I am the manager of this Tee-Ball team. Our team name is The _____ (whatever name the league assigns for your team).

      This is my first time as a Tee-Ball manager/head coach, but I have coached 1 year of AYSO soccer (add any coaching experience that you have done in the past). This is my 5 year old son _____, who will be playing on this team.

Parents Expectations of Coach:
(These are the things that a parent can hope to see taught, coached and covered by you.) :
• Teach basic baseball skills.
• Maintain a positive attitude.
• Be on time for the practices and the games,
• Demonstrate good sportsmanship at all times.

The Coach's Expectations of Parents & Players:
(These are the things that you hope to see demonstrated by the parents.) :
Be <u>on time</u> for practices and *early* for games. If you must leave early for either one let me know. If someone other than yourself will be picking up your child let me know. With all due respect, <u>I am NOT a babysitter.</u>

Every player must let me know his or her parent is present before leaving. (This is very important! It's an incredibly scary feeling to look around and not see one of your players and wonder if their parent scooped them up without informing you).

Positive Attitudes & Encouragement (for both parents & players)
Good Sportsmanship (again for both parents & players)
Treat me, as you would expect to be treated, with <u>respect</u>.

Please remember that I am a volunteer and not a paid coach.
(Yes, the parents may pay a league fee for their player, but you don't receive any of the money. So they can't say, "I pay your salary!").

Equipment / Uniform:
Cleats are recommended, but not mandatory.
(Stress that the correct equipment is safer and more productive. Keep in mind that some families may not be able to afford buying new shoes at home, let alone baseball cleats that their player will quickly grow out of).

Jerseys & caps are provided by the league. (Decide as a team what color baseball pants & socks to purchase to go long with the jersey and cap colors.) The baseball pants can normally be found at a local

Walmart or sporting goods store without breaking the bank.

Each player should bring their own **batting helmet** to avoid using a teammate's helmet. (There are hygiene issues to consider, such as common head lice.)

Each player should bring their own **water** bottles to practice and especially to the games. Players must stay hydrated so that the heat from the sun and from their physical exertion doesn't adversely affect them. Coach, it is a good idea if you bring extra water bottles for those that do forget.

Practices and Games:
Practice twice a week for 1 hour before the season starts, then once a week for 1 hour after season starts. (Ask parents to vote on a mutually agreed upon day and time.) The league will assign you a baseball field for practice and playing games.
Also, remind the parents that it is very important that they also practice with their player at home. We have all heard the adage, "Practice makes perfect." (And if it doesn't, it can't hurt.)

2 Games per week: One midweek game & one every Saturday (Schedule to be announced as soon as it's released by the League).

Positions:
At this age many of the children tend to leave their 'assigned' position and run after the ball. We will work on field positions, proper techniques and practice baseball drills. **We will rotate positions every game.** At this age it's important that the players get a chance to play each position. This allows them to see which positions they like and are able to actually play.

We will try to get players in the position that best suits them and the team. (Not every child can effectively or safely play first base or be a shortstop.)
Some players will be moving up to the next division next season and need to be prepared.

3 Pitch Rule: Hitting the ball initially starts on the batting Tee, but actual pitching from the coach typically starts well before mid-season.
Typical League Rule: Batters are to receive <u>3 pitches only.</u> If they miss hitting the ball onto the field, then place the baseball onto the batting tee. This rule applies even if the player repeatedly fouls off the ball. It's designed to keep both the game moving and the kids interested. Parents will say, "Give little [Insert name here, ex: Johnny] one more chance. He almost had it". But you are the manager. It is your team and these are the league rules. Little Johnny, or Suzy, etc, will get plenty of chances in practice and during the multiple games ahead.

Additional Coaches:

Here's where you request help from the parents on your team. Ask for an Assistant Coach, or a few coaches, to help run drills, to act as base coaches, etc. Some parents may not have wanted the responsibility of managing the whole team, but they may be willing to help out as an assistant coach. You should receive plenty of help. Parents like to stand near their player on the field as a fun memory that they can share with their child.

Once you have help you can <u>delegate duties</u>. For example, assign one of the assistant coaches to watch for Player Safety. This is especially important during batting drills. His job is to watch to make sure a player is not walking up behind you or the batter who is about to swing the bat.

The Player Safety Coach keeps an eye on all of the players while you are busy instructing, demonstrating and teaching. You can't see everything and an extra set of eyes really comes in handy.

Request a Team Mom/Team Parent (TM/TP):

Here's again where you request help from the parents. Request a parent to help out with a few planning duties that come up during the season.

<u>Team Mom/Team Parent Responsibilities</u> include things such as - Organizes the team banner,

creates refreshment schedule for games, collects candy fundraiser money to be turned in to the league, handles trophy ordering, sets up the "end of season" team party, passes along information from the manager to the parents, etc.

In most leagues parents donate money to create a vinyl banner with the team's name and mascot-type picture on it. The Team Mom/Parent calls around to the local sign/banner makers, gets an estimate, informs the parents, and then collects the money and orders the team banner. The Team Mom/Parent also brings the banner to every game.

For refreshments, each parent is typically assigned a game day to bring light, healthy, refreshing snacks for each player. These snacks can be things like Ziploc-style bags of orange slices, small boxes of raisins, or apple slices, along with a juice box or small store-bought water bottles, etc.

Hopefully the TM/TP will have some on hand in their car just in case the assigned parent forgets or does not show up for that game.

Also in most leagues at the end of the season each player gets a participation trophy at a team party to remember the season. And again the TM/TP calls around to the local trophy makers, gets an estimate, informs the parents and then collects the money and orders the trophies. They do the same for arranging a team party. It can be at a local pizza place or at a local park, with everyone bringing food and drinks potluck style.

At this first team meeting add into your closing remarks that you welcome any feedback and suggestions to make this a really fun season for everyone and to remember that, **"This is for the kids**." We signed them up so they would have fun, so let's not put any undue pressure or unrealistic expectations on them. Keep in mind the players just want to have a good time while playing a sport and we, as parents and coaches, also want them to have fun. So let the players just be kids! Life is challenging enough, why place stress on the kids over a game?!
Keep it light and keep it FUN!!!

Questions/Comments/Adjournment of the meeting:
At this time some of the parents may have a few questions. Most often they will just thank you for coaching/managing the team. You can meet the players and get their names and experience levels here too. The league should provide you with contact information (email, phone numbers) for the parents of each member on your team.
Good job Coach! That first meeting was a big step and it is now out of the way. Let's move on.

CHAPTER TWO - How To...
Tell, Show, Observe

When coaching your players at practice, always try to instruct (**Tell**) them first, secondly demonstrate (**Show**) the instruction you gave and have one of the players perform the instruction before getting everyone else involved. Then watch (**Observe)** them and correct each player as necessary.

Remember to give lots of positive encouragement and feedback during practices and during the games. The players like to hear when they have done something well. It's okay to give correction in techniques but don't be critical. Also make sure that you are not just focused on one or two players all the time. Give instruction and praise evenly to all of the players including your own player.

Coaching Philosophy

Tee-ball is meant to be a purely instructional baseball division. With that said, my coaching philosophy is simple: Have fun, show good sportsmanship and try to win (even though no score is kept in non-competitive tee-ball). Trying to **WIN** while showing good **Sportsmanship** and having **Fun** is what healthy competition is all about. Try to be easy going and don't get stressed out. Think about what YOUR coaching philosophy is and then share it with others.

Remember to give lots of praise to ALL of your players and don't forget about your own child. Do not be harder on them because they are the coaches child. Too often coaches overlook their own child in an attempt to not show some sort of favoritism. But this is your child's season also. Have fun with them and enjoy these life memories that will last many years.

Attention Span

Let's face it, young kids do not have a very long attention span. Try to be entertaining while you are instructing your players. Keep the verbal instructions relatively short, as kids do not want to hear a lecture. Also stress "safety" on your team. Explain to the players that they could accidentally get hurt if they are not paying attention. For example, they could be hit by the ball or run over by the runner on the opposing team if they are busy digging in the grass/dirt (depending on the condition of your outfield). I tell my team that one of my biggest Coach's rules is "**No playing in the grass/dirt**". The only time they should touch the grass or dirt is to field a ground ball.

One of our goals, as coaches, is to ensure that every player is safe. One way to do this is by making sure they are paying attention at <u>all times</u> during the games and the practices, even while sitting on the bench.

While we definitely want the kids to have **fun** and learn the "**FUN**damentals" of baseball, we also want them to give their _best effort_ and that includes paying attention. Baseball is fun, but it also requires _discipline_. This is a life lesson for the players also.

As coaches we will gladly give cheers when the players deserve it and offer encouragement when the kids need it, but we will also bring any mistakes to their attention so they can learn from their mistakes. Make sure you do this in a positive manner. Never lose your patience and never embarrass any of your players. If they make a mistake, do not make a big deal out of it. Credit them for trying and then simply show them how they could have handled the situation better. You might say, "That was a nice effort, Billy, but try this next time…"

We are not doing our job as coaches if we allow the kids to goof off during a game or practice. We do not want anyone to get injured because they weren't watching the ball or another player. Teach them that there is no swinging the bat wildly also (See Chapter Three : Bat Safety). The only time they should swing a bat is when they are standing at the baseball tee. That includes during both practices and games.

Dealing with the Assistant Coaches and Parents in General

Having assistant coaches assist on your team does not mean that you will lose control or authority over your team. You are the Head Coach/Manager of your team. Typically in all of professional sports there are several coaches involved with a team. And remember there are going to be a lot of excited parents who want to feel as though they are a part of their son/daughter's first year or second year of tee-ball. Welcome their help, as they can also help you keep an eye on the kids.

Make sure you always have a good idea of what you will cover during practice (See Drill Ideas in Chapter 8). That way no one else can "take over" your practice. Let your coaches know what you want to cover and break up the team into smaller groups to work on drills using these assistant coaches. Be organized by having an order to your practices with specific drills written down on a paper or electronic device, such as a tablet or a smartphone. This can really make a difference between having an effective, fun practice or a disorganized, boring practice.

You may eventually find yourself faced with a 'problem' parent. You know, one who is either critical of the job you are doing, always has suggestions of how they "would run things," or always questions why their child does not get to play first base every game. But they did not offer to coach the team in the beginning, remember?!

Pull this parent aside and remind them that you are just a volunteer and a parent also. You are doing the best job you can and if they would like to suggest something helpful you would be happy to listen. Keep your cool and by talking with them one on one, this will usually disarm the problem parent.

For the latter situation about preferred position, explain that, at the tee-ball age it is very important to rotate all of the players through all of the positions. As they move up in the divisions, then they may be placed in one primary position that best suits the team. But for now your goal is to be fair to the entire team. Plus their child will benefit and be a well-rounded player by playing the entire field.

If the parent continues to be disruptive, call your Division Representative/Director of Managers, (the person in charge of the tee-ball teams in your league), fill them in on the situation and then let them handle this person.

You want and *deserve* to have fun like everyone else on your team. You should <u>not</u> try to placate a complainer just to silence them. Have an open mind, but stand firm if you feel you are right. The other parents on your team will see this and they will respect you even more. Take the matter to a league representative for help if the problem persists.

Be Prepared

You can do this for practices also, but before every game make a list of the players' names and what position you will put them in for each inning of the game (typically 3 innings for tee-ball). Also create a batting lineup so the players know what order they will bat in. This can all be listed on one sheet of paper and it doesn't have to be a piece of artwork. Or you could buy a small dry erase marker board at most sporting goods stores to post in your dugout for the entire team to see. Either way, just list every position and then the players' names next to each position. Remember to rotate after each inning, so the same kids do not get stuck in the outfield trying to pick daisies.

For the players too young to read well, tell the players to look at the person sitting in front of them on the bench to remember their batting order for the entire game. These are their "bench buddies" for the game. All players bat through the line-up each inning.

Field Position Names and Position Numbers (*For your reference*) :

POSITION	POSITION NUMBER
Pitcher...	1
Catcher...	2
1st Base...	3
2nd Base...	4
3rd Base...	5
Shortstop...	6
Left Fielder...	7
Center Fielder...	8
Right Fielder...	9

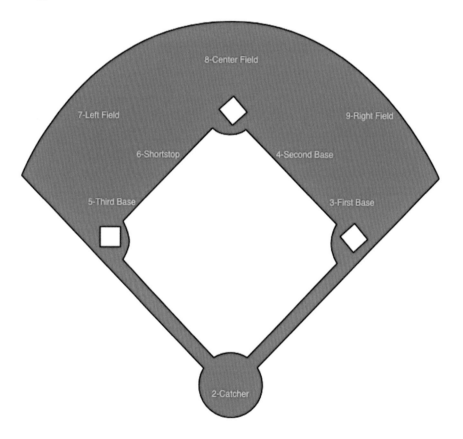

In youth baseball you might have between 12-15 players assigned to your team by the league. This is primarily because some players either don't show up for one or multiple games (depending on their parent's work schedule, life circumstances, etc) or they simply quit the team before the end of the season. So when fielding more than the normal 9 players on your baseball team you will want to use a "Floater" or "Rover" between 1st and 2nd base and 2 center field positions (right-center & left-center).

The pitcher stands within the chalked "Pitcher's circle". So with extra players use 2 pitchers standing apart from one another in the "Pitcher's Circle" and fill any other gaps with extra players if you have them.

Show your players the field and walk them to each position. Remember most of these kids have never even stepped onto a baseball field before. Also show them where the Pitcher, Catcher, Short Stop and the Outfielders will stand.

During the first several practices as a warmup, run the bases by leading your players in the correct base order. If you were to just tell your team to run the bases, some kids will accidentally start to run the opposite way (from Home Plate towards Third Base), both during practice and during an actual game. This is ok; they are learning. Laugh it off and calmly instruct them to run in the correct direction.

As your players run the bases have them loudly call out each base by name as they touch it. For example: "First base, Second base, Third Base,

Home Plate!" It is fun for them and it will reinforce the order of the bases and the direction to run.

Run the bases!

CHAPTER THREE
Team Rules

As the Manager or Head Coach of the team you need to set and enforce rules for your team. Do not make it too complicated. You only need a couple of rules, but let the kids know what the rules are from the very first practice. Be consistent; If it is a rule on day one then it is a rule all season. The first Team rule you probably should cover is "Bat Safety" because right away the players are going to want to swing a bat. And normally they do this when they are standing too close to others.

Bat Safety

1. <u>Do not</u> pick up a bat or swing a bat unless instructed to do so by your coach. No player is even allowed to pick up a bat without wearing a batting helmet.
2. No other players should be in the immediate vicinity of any batter! Inform your players to look around before they swing a bat. Safety First!

3. Always be aware of other people around you **before swinging the bat.** Especially in practice when other kids may be walking up to or around the batter's box.

Remind your hitters of this during games especially when there is a catcher. Some players will want to take a few "warm-up" swings as they approach home plate. But they need to remember that there is a catcher behind them who might not be paying attention and who may be standing too close to them. So always be aware and LOOK before you swing; even a warm up swing!

Pay Attention

1. No playing in the dirt!!!

We covered this under "Attention Span" in chapter two. Explain to your players that sometimes *they will be bored*, but that you do not allow your team to play with pebbles, dirt, flowers, etc. They need to watch the ball as much as possible. If they are bored in the outfield have them do chants, such as, "Hey batter, batter, batter. Hey batter, batter, batter" to keep them 'in the game'.

5. No laughing at teammates or members of the other team if someone makes a mistake. (This is teaching good sportsmanship).

Each player is bound to make mistakes, but that is what learning is all about. We can laugh "with" our teammates, but not "at" them. If it's funny and appropriate to do so, then all the players should be laughing, but never at the expense of only one or two players.

No Umpires

In tee-ball you don't use actual umpires. Since you are the one that will be placing the ball on the batting tee for your batters to hit, then you will act as the home plate umpire. Your assistant coaches will act as the field umpires watching the action on the field and at each of the bases.

As we already discussed in Chapter One (3 Pitch Rule), hitting the ball initially starts on the batting Tee, but actual pitching from the coach to the batter typically starts well before mid-season. So, as your players continue to develop their baseball hitting skills, you (and your assistant coaches) will be pitching the ball to the batters instead of using the batting tee.

Typical League Rule: Batters are to receive 3 pitches only. If they miss hitting the ball onto the field, then place the baseball on the batting tee. This rule applies even if the player repeatedly fouls off the ball. Remind your players that if they miss their 3 pitches, not to be upset, and that it is okay to use the tee. They will get plenty of chances to hit a coach-pitched ball in their next practice and during their future games.

CHAPTER FOUR - *Catch and Throw*
The Catch

Teach your players how to catch the ball whether its high or low. Instruct them to use both their glove hand and their free hand and to remember two words...**Pinkies** & **Thumbs**.

If the ball is above your waist, you put your thumbs together to form a **"W"** with your palms facing away from you.

If the ball is below your waist, you put your little fingers (pinkies) together to form an **"M"** with your fingers pointed down and your palms facing out. First, demonstrate this without a baseball glove on so the players can see the letters "W" & "M," and then show them with the glove on.

If catching a fly ball on a sunny day, show your players how holding the glove up above their heads and faces can block the sun out of their eyes. Remind them not to look up directly at the sun (yes, sometimes young children do this without thinking ahead of time).

Position Your Body - The Ready Position

Tell the players to always try to catch the ball near the middle of their body. To do this they must move their feet in the direction of the throw or hit. That means moving forward, backwards or to the side.

A lot of young players will just stick their glove out and reach out away from them because they are afraid of getting hit with the ball. Explain to your players that if they get under the ball for a pop fly or behind it for a line drive and get their glove in front of the ball they won't be hit by it. It's often when they shy away from the ball that they are most likely to get hit by it.

A good suggestion is to throw tennis balls up into the air during practice at first. This will help your players get used to catching pop-ups and will lessen any pain in case they miss the catch and do get hit with the ball.

When fielding grounders, point your open glove down so that it's actually **touching the dirt**, and trap the ball into your glove with your free hand. All too often the young player does not get his glove down low enough and the ball rolls right under his glove and through his legs.

I have included a drill that I often used called, "Shuffle, Shuffle, Dirt" to practice fielding grounders. (See Chapter Eight : "Drill Ideas".)

The Throw

After the ball is caught using both hands (or one hand for the more experienced players), the arms should be brought to the "throwing position" as quickly as possible.

Teach the players to **point**, **step** and **throw**. Here's what I mean. The player should immediately separate their glove hand and their throwing hand. They move the throwing arm with the ball to the throwing position with the arm cocked back and the elbow bent. Then point their glove hand at their teammate that they will be throwing to (such as first base of the catcher). Follow that by stepping towards their teammate with their 'stride' foot (the foot opposite of the hand holding the ball) and then throw the ball and follow through by stepping forward with that back leg. Pointing the glove at their target also helps the player maintain his/her balance while throwing the ball.
Teach your players to only throw the ball to another player if they are paying attention and actively looking and waiting for the throw.

Gripping the Baseball

This may be a little advanced for the younger players, but if you have a second-year tee-ball player, he/she should hear this instruction anyway to be prepared for the next division up.

1) Place forefinger and middle finger close, but not together, and across the seams (stitching) of the baseball.

2) The thumb is placed underneath the ball and between the top two fingers thereby providing support for the throw.

3) There should be a slight space between the palm and the ball. Also, the remaining fingers should be bent slightly to the side of the ball.

Demonstrate this first for all of your players and then have them do it. Have them stay on the baseline and walk down the line of players and check each grip visually.

CHAPTER FIVE - All About Batting
Up at Bat

The only 2 players to even hold a bat are the current batter at the plate and the player "on deck" (the next batter up) – everyone else stays seated on the bench in their assigned batting order.

Since you will be busy setting up the batting tee (& eventually pitching to the players) and your assistant coaches will be at 1st & 3rd base, have your Team Mom/Parent keep the players in their correct batting order or have an extra helper/assistant coach do it.

Explain to your players that when they swing the bat they should envision the ball sitting on top of a table. To hit the ball off the table they will need to swing "nice and level". If they swing down on the ball they will be chopping up the table and the ball will not be hit properly. So, tell them 'no chopping wood'! Also, no upward 'golf swings', just a nice and level motion.

Choose Your "Thunder-Stick"

Choosing the correct bat (length and weight) is very important. Players will oftentimes grab a bat that is too heavy or big for them. Here is a way to help them choose the right bat.

The player should be able to grab and hold the bat straight out in front of them with one hand for 10-15 seconds. If it dips heavily or falls down, then the bat is simply too heavy for them. Besides, explain that a thinner or lighter bat may provide increased bat speed for him/her, which can result in better hitting.

Only Little League approved bats having a maximum 2 1⁄4" inch diameter are allowed. Big Barrel Bats are NOT allowed at this level for safety reasons.

The Stance

The parallel or squared stance is typically recommended for young players. The batter basically has both toes of their feet equal distance from home plate. Also, the batter's feet should be positioned a little more than shoulder width apart. The batter should have a slight bend in the knees and the bat should not rest on the shoulders. Keep that bat up and active, ready to swing, not resting on vacation.

Knock-Knock Grip

The grip on the bat should be comfortable and ideally the middle **("knock-knock")** knuckles on each hand should line up. This helps in executing the proper swing without over-rotating the wrists.

I ask my players to pretend they are knocking on a door so they can see which knuckles I am referring to. The larger knuckles on the very top of the hand should not be lined up or their wrists are

over rotated and are too tense for an efficient swing and follow through.

Where Should the Back Elbow Be?

For tee-ball players the elbows should be *relaxed*. Contrary to what a lot of first time tee-ball/baseball coaches say, you do NOT need to raise the back elbow. Quite often, coaches and parents yell, "Keep that back elbow up Billy" (Insert name here). Raising the back elbow just creates

more tension in the swinging motion.
Instead you should create an upside down "V" with the hands and the arms.

The back elbow should be in a relaxed position for these young players, without unnecessary tension in the shoulder. The back elbow should <u>never</u> be above the hands. Now for the older players who will be moving up into a higher division next season who feel that raising the elbow gives them more power, then they can raise the elbow of their top hand to be *parallel* with the shoulder.

Remind your players to keep their hands together on the bat with their "knock-knock" knuckles lined up.

Load and Stride

To "load" means to shift some of your weight onto your back leg (the leg furthest from the pitcher) and pull your hands back slightly as you prepare to swing the bat at the ball. Once pitching (typically from the manager or coaches) begins, tell your players to "load up" when they see the pitcher's arm start to come forward with the ball. If they wait to load until after the ball is released, they may not have enough time to swing.

To "stride" simply take a small step towards the pitcher with the front leg as you hit the ball to increase the force of the swing. Try to keep your hands and weight back during your stride. Swing once your front foot lands, not while it is still off of the ground. This provides more power coming from the legs and hips. Hitting is not just about using your arms and hands.

At first your players will not really grasp these technical instructions, but with plenty of repetition and practice, they will eventually understand them and they will be able to accomplish these movements in fluid motion.

Squash the Bug

Tell your players to keep their back foot (not the foot facing the pitcher) on the ground and "**squash the bug**" as they swing. This is accomplished by pivoting the foot around and not lifting the toes off the ground, essentially squashing a pretend bug underneath their shoe. This will give them more batting power and balance.

Watch the Ball

Make sure your players watch the ball, not the pitcher, and tell them to <u>not</u> turn their head and "pose" for a picture at third base. Here's what I mean. Young players have a habit of turning their head early as they swing the bat and end up looking at the third baseman. The batter should be looking down the barrel of the bat, actually watching **the bat hit the ball.**

At the end of the swing the player's belly button should be facing the pitcher. This demonstrates proper rotation of the hips after swinging the bat. Frequently remind them to "Watch the ball" and to "Look down the barrel".

Don't Throw the Bat!

Young players have a tendency to throw the bat at the end of their swing. They do this out of excitement and because they don't realize they are doing it at first. Instruct them to simply "drop the bat" behind them or off to the side after they have hit the ball. Demonstrate this to them in slow motion on how to do this. Remember to "Tell, Show and then Observe" (covered in Chapter Two).

I have seen bats accidentally thrown after swinging, into a crowd of family supporters at more than one game. It can be a very scary experience, trust me. Batting helmets for the audience wouldn't be a bad idea for the first few games!

I recommend waiting a few games before you start using a player in the catcher position due to the initial bat throwing tendencies. When you do start using a catcher, have him/her *always* wear a batting helmet and for several games have them stand off to the side, *Not* directly behind home plate like a normal catching position. (Preferably on the right side of the plate for a right-handed batter and left side for a left-handed batter to avoid any flying bats.)

If they are a right-handed batter they will tend to throw the bat with their left hand at the end of the swinging motion. Therefore, the bat will typically be thrown to the left side for a right-handed batter and to the right side for a left-handed batter. Then once the players learn to not do this and the bat throwing stops, you can allow the catcher to stand directly behind home plate and the batter.

CHAPTER SIX - About the Bases
Foul & Fair

Teach your players that a FOUL ball is any ball going out of the baselines before going past 1st or 3rd base. If the ball hits either 1st or 3rd base and goes out of the field it is considered a FAIR ball and should be played.

The ball is also FAIR if the ball stops ON the line before passing 1st or 3rd base. The ball may even roll out of the baseline and swerve back onto the field to be considered FAIR, as long as it's before 1st or 3rd base. If it rolls out and then back onto the field beyond 1st or 3rd base it is a FOUL ball.

The ball is considered FAIR if a fielding player touches the baseball in the air in fair territory, but then either drops it, or deflects the ball into foul territory. But the ball is a FOUL ball if the fielding player attempts to catch it and touches it while in foul territory but then drops it.

Base Running

The batter after getting a hit becomes a runner. As a runner, he/she may over-run 1st base _only_ without being "tagged out". So, if they were to run from 1st base to 2nd base and step off of 2nd because they over ran it, then they can be tagged out by an opposing player in possession of the ball.

See my drill "Take One" in Chapter Eight to practice over-running first base. When the batter hits a single (first base only), he/she must hustle as quickly as possible to first base. Make sure your runner isn't slowing down as he/she approaches first base, but rather does not slow down until after stepping on 1st base and even past it.

Make sure your players know that when they are running the bases they must tag every base and home plate. You will be amazed at how many times your players will step over a base or miss the corner of a base while rounding it while running to the next base.

A good warmup is to have your team run the bases at the beginning of practice to get their adrenaline pumping and to get them comfortable with the bases. Again, as mentioned at the end of Chapter 2, instruct the kids to call out the name of each base and home plate as they step on them ("First base, Second base, Third base, Home plate").

Remind your players to 'pump' their arms back and forth as they run for momentum and to lean forward slightly instead of running in a totally upright position.

No Blocking (Bases or Home Plate)

Also make sure your defensive players on all bases and at home plate know that they cannot block the base or home plate unless they have the ball (See Chapter Seven "Throw to the Catcher" and Chapter Eight for "Force Out," etc.). If they do not have the ball to make a play to get the runner out, then they must move out of the runners way so he is unobstructed.

In non-competitive leagues there is no base stealing or leading-off from the base. The runners must touch each base with their foot until the ball is hit from the opposing team. Check with your league regarding these rules for any rule changes in your area.

Using Base Coaches

Here's another area where your assistant coaches come into play. Have one coach stand at 1st base and the other at 3rd. Instruct your players to listen to the 1st base coach after getting a hit. The 1st base coach will tell them to run to 2nd ("Take two") or stay at 1st. The 3rd base coach will do the same by instructing them to either stay at second base or run to third and possibly even home plate. Remind your players to look over at the 3rd base coach as they get to 2nd base for the instruction to either stay there or to keep running.

Fielding Ground Balls

When 'fielding' the players should ideally be in the "ready" position. The ready position involves the players spreading their feet slightly wider than shoulder width while bending at the back leaning slightly forward with their seat (butt) down and their hands in front of them. Their hands stay active and ready to catch the ball.

Remember to tell them, "Glove in the dirt," when fielding grounders so that the ball doesn't roll under their glove.

Base Coverages

Certain playing positions on the field cover other playing positions. For example: the shortstop (SS) covers both the third and second baseman. If the Third or Second baseman leaves their position to run forward towards a ground ball then the SS runs to cover their base to receive a throw in order to get "out" any runner headed to that base.

Consequently, the Outfield positions back up the Infield positions. For example: the Centerfielder

(CF) covers the Pitcher. If the Pitcher misses a hit ball, the CF runs forward to field (retrieve) the hit ball. The Right Fielder (RF) covers the First Baseman because the Second Baseman needs to stay near his base in order to make a play. If the First baseman leaves his position to run forward towards a hit ground ball then the RF runs to cover 1st base to receive a throw in order to get "out" any runner headed to 1st base.

It will take many practices and several actual games until your players start to get the concept of covering bases. At first most of your players will automatically run after the same hit ball, leaving their positions. But eventually they will learn to stay in their assigned positions if they are not actually near the hit ball or are not really involved in the play. Again, just laugh because sometimes it is funny and remain patient as a good coach does.

Be Alert...Charge!

You will need to remind your players to be ready and aware of the current base runner situation quite often. In non-competitive leagues, there is no "3 outs" rule, as everyone in the lineup bats straight through. Therefore, the players should know where the runners are (whether on first base and third or on first base only, etc.), and what to do with the ball when it comes to them.

Instruct your team to be aggressive defensively. When on the field they need to go after the ball. Instruct them to **"Charge"** the ball and not simply wait for it to come to them. If they keep their feet moving or even just rock side to side on their legs then they will be more ready to move towards the ball. This way they are ready to run forward towards a ground ball or to get underneath a pop fly ball.

Also remind all of your players to *be alert*. Especially the pitcher(s) standing in the pitching circle. They shouldn't be standing flat-footed. As I've mentioned the outfielders should be ready to move somewhere on the field, either straight to the ball, or to back up an infielder who is fielding the ball. This way they are ready to back up an infielder who might miss a ball that was thrown or hit to him.

While on defense on the field, tell your players to turn and watch every 'hit' ball even if they are not involved in the play. This is so they know where the ball is at all times and so they don't accidentally get hit in the head when a teammate behind them tries to throw it to the pitcher or to a baseman.

CHAPTER SEVEN - *Where to Throw the Ball*
Throw to First...

Teach your players the basic fielding and throwing sequence: Infielders throw the ball to 1st base, outfielders throw to second base. If the ball makes it to the outfield, your outfielders will not have enough time to field it and then throw it to first base in time to make a play by getting the batter out at first. They should instinctively, with plenty of practice, throw it to second base to make the play.

Throw to the Catcher...

When using a catcher, get your team used to the idea of throwing to him/her. For example, quite often the ball will be thrown to first base in an effort to make a play. After the 1st baseman gets the ball and has stepped on his base to get the runner out, he should throw to the catcher if there is a runner on 3rd base headed to home plate for a possible double play. During practice do this over and over even if you do not have a runner on third base. This keeps your catcher involved in the practice a lot more also.

Another time the catcher is very busy is during "last batter" in non-competitive tee-ball. Coaches should announce "Last batter" when the last player up to bat approaches the plate. Once the batter gets a hit, he and everyone ahead of him runs around the bases <u>without stopping</u>. The fielding team can still try to get as many runners 'out' as possible; this applies especially to the catcher when his teammates might have missed tagging the runners.

Have your catcher stand in front of home plate on the third baseline and tag out the incoming runner(s). Remember to instruct your players that if the catcher (or any baseman) is not receiving the ball or does not have possession of the ball, he *must* move, so as not to impede the runners from touching home plate. This goes for your basemen also. There should be NO blocking of the bases or home plate without the ball. (See Chapter Six: "No Blocking").

Nobody moves 'on or off' the field while the "last batter" is still running to home plate. Wait for the runner to cross home plate. This again is to show good sportsmanship to all runners. The last runner will be excited to run to home plate just like any other player and should get that thrill without bumping into players leaving the field.

When in Doubt…Throw the Ball to the Pitcher

Tell your players, if they get confused and don't know exactly where to throw the ball, or if the runners are already at a base, to throw the ball to the pitcher to end the play. When the ball is thrown to the pitcher the runners must stop at the base closest to them. Tell your players to not hold onto the ball. For fun, you could have the kids play "Hot potato" with the ball during a practice to get used to getting rid of the ball quickly. And obviously the pitcher needs to remain alert at all times during practice and especially during the game.

Force Out Play

A "**Forced out**" is when a player is "*forced*" to run to the next base because the batter advances to first base after a hit. A runner on 1st base is "forced" to run to 2nd. Consequently, a runner already on 2nd would then be "forced" to run to 3rd. In this instance the fielding player only has to get the ball and touch the base before the runner touches it to get the runner out. But if it is not a "forced out" situation, you have to tag the runner with the ball before he touches the base in order to get him out.

Double Play

Teach your players to always try to make a double play. If the ball is hit to the short stop and there is a runner on 1st and 2nd, he should try to tag the runner going by him with the ball if possible (remember the runner on second is 'forced' to run to third base), then throw to 1st or 2nd base for a double play. The same plan goes for any infield position. Try to tag any runner when possible and then throw to a base the next runner is headed towards.

Or if one of your players catches a fly ball, he/she should then look for a base to throw to in order to get a runner out, (see *Fly Out*).

Fly Out

If you are a runner on any base and you run to the next base as your teammate hits a "pop fly" (or any hit ball like a "line drive" that doesn't touch the ground) **that is caught**, you must return to your original base to avoid a double play. The player who hit the caught pop fly/hit ball is automatically out. So any base runner must return to the base they were originally on. If they don't and the defensive baseman throws the ball back to their original base, then that baseman steps on the base and they are automatically out.

For example: The runner on 1st base runs to 2nd base after his teammate hits a pop fly into the air. The pop fly is caught, say by the shortstop. If the runner does not return to 1st base before the shortstop throws the ball to the 1st baseman who steps on (or tags) the base, then the runner is automatically out.

This is a tough one to get the kids to understand because they want to run full force to the next base. It takes at least half a season to get them to watch a pop fly on the run before racing all the way to the next base.

Field Rotation

At practices you want to rotate all of the kids through the positions and believe me that can get confusing with 12 or more players on your team. Here's the system I use so that I know everyone has fairly rotated through each position: the outfield players rotate to their right and the infield rotates left.

For example, when practicing batting have each player take 5 hits off of the batting tee (or pitch to them if they've mastered the tee) and run to 1st base on the 5th hit only. This reinforces to the hitter to run through first base! See my drill "Take One" in Chapter Eight to practice over-running first base.

The runner then puts his batting helmet away, grabs his glove and goes to right field. The right fielder moves to his right over to center field, the center fielder moves over to left field and the left fielder goes to play 3rd base. The 3rd baseman moves to his left to short stop, the short stop moves to his left to 2nd base, 2nd baseman moves to his left to 1st base. The 1st baseman moves to the pitcher's spot and the pitcher is the next to bat. The movement is like a big "S" snake. You do not use a catcher for this drill.

Good Sportsmanship

To show good sportsmanship and to avoid any arguments, in a game the Visiting team bats first and the Home team bats last. Check your game schedule before each game to see if you are listed as 'Home' or 'Visitor.' Also, the Home team is expected to prepare the field for play. That may mean chalking the baselines, laying out the bases, picking up any rocks/trash/debris off the field, etc., before the game.

Again this is where your assistant coaches can be of great help. You shouldn't have to do everything yourself. Make sure you ask for help ahead of time. Be a good delegator of duties because you're going to be busy enough.

The Visitors are expected to clean up the field after the game. This would include putting the bases away in a league provided storage shed, disposing of any trash/debris (like lots of half-empty water bottles) left behind by the spectators & players and generally making sure the field looks as presentable, or even better, than it did before the game started.

At the end of each game assemble your team in a circle and cheer for the other team. For example, "Two, four, six, eight, who do we appreciate? Padres!" And then have your team form a single file line and walk forward to shake hands (or slap a high-five) with each hand of the opponent. This promotes good sportsmanship and with non-competitive tee-ball both teams win anyway no matter what the score was!

Another Word on Demonstrating Good Sportsmanship

Your players, their parents and all game attendees will be watching you and your actions. The players will learn from and copy your good example. Make sure that you leave your ego off the field and demonstrate good sportsmanship to the other team, coaches and parents regardless of the final score. This is a teaching/learning level in Little League baseball. You are helping build character in your players. Kids will remember their coaches for many years to come. You want them to have fond memories of you Coach. And your son/daughter and your family will be proud of the way that you conducted yourself.

Remember that if you witness any bad sportsmanship you can report any problems to your league representatives.

Hi-5's Only, Coach

In today's society there is necessary heightened awareness and help for preventing child abuse/molestation. But because of this serious subject, as coaches we must be very careful with how we behave and interact with and around the kids. For example, we should no longer pat them on the behind after a good play, as this may appear inappropriate to many parents even if the intention is harmless.

I recommend simply to high-five your players after a good play. To avoid any misunderstandings or possible false accusations, make sure you are never alone with any player from your team, excluding your own son/daughter of course. If a parent drops their player off for a practice or a game and is late picking them up, ask another parent, preferably of your opposite sex, to stay and wait with you and that player. It's always smart to have a witness, if you will, to avoid any problems.

And of course no swearing, smoking, drinking alcohol, etc. It is all common sense stuff. Be on your best behavior as if someone was filming you because with all of the smartphones and mini cameras today they probably are.

As with anything else in life, if you do not do anything wrong, you won't have anything to worry about. Enough said.

CHAPTER EIGHT - Drill ideas
Take One

❖   As we have stated earlier under "Base Running" in Chapter Six, the runner can only over-run 1st base without being "tagged out". A good drill for teaching this is to have your assistant coach stand about 3-5 feet past the first base on the baseline. Then have your team line up in single file and tell the first runner to "Take One". That means that he/she should pretend they have only hit a single and need to get to first base <u>as fast as they can</u>.

     The runner should run to first, touch first base and keep running until they have 'high-fived' or slapped the baseline coach's hand. This reinforces to them to not slow down until they have run "through" the base. They can then take a few chopping steps to slow down and then return to first base just like in a real game.

     The first runner then goes to the end of the line and the next player runs on your signal. Repeat this several times with each runner before moving on to the next drill.

Throwing & Catching Drills

❖ Have players stand side by side (with a generous spacing in between them) and then form a second line with the players facing each other. Vary the distance that you space each line apart as your players become more competent at throwing and catching the ball.

Stress good throws and remind the team that it doesn't matter how hard they can throw the ball if it doesn't go straight to their teammate. Too often they want to throw hard, but miss their target completely. Accuracy is more important at this stage than just their arm throwing strength.

❖ Players form a giant circle and throw the ball to each other. Tell them they cannot throw it directly back to the player that threw the ball to them. Rotate where the players stand in the circle to ensure everyone gets the ball a lot. Also after one round, speed them up. You want your players to decide whom to throw to and then get rid of the ball quickly.

Shuffle, Shuffle, Dirt (SSD)

❖ Players form one line standing side by side (spaced generously) and get in the "ready position". At your instruction of "Shuffle, shuffle, dirt " everyone shuffles to their left and then pretends to field a ground ball from the center of their body with their glove touching the dirt/ground. Then return to the 'ready position' and repeat.

SSD teaches them how to move over into the path of the ball and then to field a grounder. Repeat in the opposite direction. Repeat numerous times.

Fielding Drill

❖ Have several players line up behind first base, 2nd base, the short stop position and 3rd base and then hit the ball to them one at a time. Make sure that your "waiting" or "next up" players in line stand well behind the first player in front of them. This will allow the first player plenty of room in case he has to back up to catch a pop fly. The first players at their positions (2nd base, the short stop position and 3rd base position) have to field a ground ball or catch the ball in the air and then make a throw to the first baseman. Your first baseman has to remain ready to receive the throw at all times.

Instruct your outfielder positions throwing to second base and third base. You can instruct the outfielders to throw to second base or third base to switch it up.

Rotate all positions (the players at 1st base go to 2nd base, the players at 2nd base go to the short stop (SS) position, etc.) Repeat this drill several times with your infield players rotating with your outfielder positions.

Double Play at Home Plate

❖   Have several players line up at the short stop, 1st base and catcher positions. Only one player participates at a time in those positions. The extra players stay back and wait for their turn. You will hit the ball while pretending that there is a batter at the plate with a runner on third base. Bat a ground ball to the short stop. He/she will field the ground ball and throw it to 1st base. The 1st baseman gets the ball and steps onto 1st base to get the imaginary runner out. The 1st baseman then throws to the catcher for a double play, getting the imaginary runner from third base out.

Rotate the catchers to the short stop position, the short stops to first base and the first basemen to the catcher position, so everyone has a chance at each position for this drill.

Incorporate the use of actual base runners after your team gets good at this drill. This adds excitement to the drill and really requires everyone to be alert and ready.

In tee-ball you will see a lot of coaches telling their runner on third base to run to home plate on *any* hit ball, (except on a pop fly that is caught, of course). Therefore, this exercise is really good at getting your catcher into the action. In non-competitive tee-ball you do not keep score, but it is still a lot of fun to see a play made at home plate.

CHAPTER NINE - Things to Know for Your Season:

This chapter covers general information that you need to know to help you with your season. It has some very common Little League tee-ball rules, but please check with your league for any minor differences. (Suggestion: Print out the official league rules and keep them with you at all times.)

Also, be sure to review the "Quick Review Workbook" located at the back of this guide.

The included workbook is meant as a Quick Review *reference tool*. You can use the workbook at any time (before leaving your house, while at practice or even during games). It covers easily reviewable reminders and information for you without having to go back to read a specific chapter.

The workbook information includes: Covering the initial team meeting, a list of delegated duties to others, practice and game responsibilities (before and after), team parent duties, field player rotation, field position numbers and more.

The league should provide your team with most of the necessary equipment such as a few team batting helmets, baseball bats, balls and a batting tee, which has an adjustable height, flexible tube, and movable base.
In tee-ball RIF (reduced injury factor) Safety Balls - level one safety baseballs (with a sponge/rubber center) Shall be used in all games and practices. They are the softest and safest ball on the market aimed at players just learning how to catch and play baseball.

Game Day Information:

• The Home team will use the first base dugout.

• The Home team is responsible for prepping the field prior to the game by chalking the first and third baselines, the pitcher's circle, the batter's boxes, (the fair ball arc if used in your league), and putting the bases into place prior to both teams taking the field for pre-game warm-ups.

Note: In some leagues the Home team will chalk a 12-foot arc, which is centered at home plate, and touches the 3rd baseline and the 1st baseline. In these leagues a batted ball must cross this arc-line to be considered a fair ball. Balls that stop short or are fielded within this arc are considered foul balls. Runners only advance on fair balls. If no arc is used in your league, then any ball hit onto the field is considered a fair ball.

- For the "Pitcher's circle" typically a ten-foot (10') diameter circle will be chalk-outlined around the pitcher's mound/area. This is where the pitcher will stand and must keep both feet completely inside of the pitcher's circle until the ball is hit.

- The Home team supplies the game balls.

- The Visiting team will use the third base dugout.

- Upon completion of the game of the day, the Visiting team will be responsible for the field cleanup and making sure that all equipment is properly stored and secured in a league provided shed or storage container.

- The Visiting team bats first.

- Games are given a time limit of 1 hour and 30 minutes from the scheduled start time or three complete innings, whichever comes first.

- No score shall be kept in tee-ball and runs and outs will not be counted.

- A completed half-inning will consist of a team batting through their entire roster with the "last batter," and any preceding runners, advancing through all four bases, (i.e., like a home run), even if the ball is caught or they are tagged out.

Batting:

- Make sure that All of your batters and runners wear a batting helmet at all times. This is a must even during practices.

- Around midseason the manager or coaches will begin "Coach Pitch". Here a coach shall pitch the baseball either gently overhand from a kneeling position or underhand from a standing position from approximately 10-15 feet away from batter.

Note: Some tee-ball leagues utilize a chalked 12-foot arc, which is centered at home plate, and touches the 3rd baseline and the 1st baseline. In these leagues a batted ball must cross this arc-line to be considered a fair ball. Balls that stop short or are fielded within this arc are considered foul balls. The ruling is a dead ball, no play, and all runners must return to their base at the time of the hit. After multiple attempts by the batter and in the interest of encouraging the batter's self-confidence and keeping the game moving, a manager may call the ball fair at their discretion. There are no strikeouts in this instructional division.
If no chalked arc is used in your league, then any ball hit onto the field is considered a fair ball.

- Any hit ball other than a home run, which goes over the perimeter fence, shall result in the runners advancing a maximum of two bases (a double).

- You can choose to alternate the batting order throughout the season for each inning so that each player eventually gets to start an inning and end an inning (acting as last batter).

- The catcher will wear a catcher's mask, shin guards, a chest protector.
  A soft protective cup is also recommended.
  A catcher's mitt is suggested, but a baseball glove may be used in the absence of one.

Base Running:

- The base runners must be have their foot in contact with the base when the ball is hit by the batter. There are no lead-offs or base stealing in tee-ball. The runner simply advances to a base on balls that are hit fairly into play.

- The Batter and any other runners can only take one (1) base on any hit ball for any reason. Example: Runners may not advance on an overthrow. When the defensive team makes an overthrow that goes out of play, the ball is considered 'dead.' This keeps the game more fun instead of having the runners just circle the bases all the way around to home plate because of inaccurate throws. The infielders and outfielders are learning too.

- A runner is automatically out when he/she purposely runs more than three (3) feet outside of a direct line between any two bases to avoid being tagged out. They are not considered out if they run outside of this direct line to avoid interfering or running into a fielder that is fielding the ball.

- There is absolutely No head-first sliding allowed for obvious safety reasons. At this age you don't even have to worry about teaching your players to slide at all in this beginning instructional division.

- After the batter hits the ball, a coach from the offensive team will move the baseball bat and the batting tee away from home plate when a player is running from third base.

- Teach your players that there are No intentional impacts at home plate or at any base. For example, this means that the runner cannot purposely run into the catcher and conversely, the catcher cannot purposely collide/impact with the runner at home plate. At this young age they won't be trying to do so anyway, but it is a good teaching point to prepare them for when they move up to the next division.

- The last batter in your line-up, (and all preceding runners), will run all the way to home plate, touching every base without stopping, after hitting the ball.

Medical Release Forms:

- The league will require that all team Managers maintain a current Medical Release form for each player.
- The Manager/Coach must have these forms in their possession of at all times during all league activities.
- Team Managers/Coaches should review Medical Release forms for all players for any special conditions that the player may have. (Example: you may have players who are allergic to bee stings.) This is good to know in case first aid or other injury treatment is needed.

Dugout Supervision:

- An assistant coach or Team Mom/Parent needs to be in the dugout at all times, while you're helping you players at bat. His/her function is to keep your players in their batting order and to maintain overall order. They can keep the seated players focused on the game and aware of who's on what base. This is also to ensure player safety within the dugout.

Regarding your Volunteers:

Volunteer Applications-
- The league will require that anyone that you have acting as assistant coaches or as a team Mom/Parent and thereby having regular,

consistent contact with the players submit a Little League Volunteer Application. The League will retain a copy of a current Drivers License or other state issued identification for the purpose of conducting a background check.

It makes sense and keeps all of the kids safe.

On Offense and Defense:

Placing Extra Players on the Field-

A. In some leagues if a team has more than eleven (11) players, they may designate that the additional players sit out during one defensive inning. (Check with your league.)

Once a player has sat out (1) one inning, he/she may not sit out again until all of your players have had their turn sitting out an inning. If this is the case in your league make sure that you keep track of who has sat and who has not so that you fairly rotate through your team.

B. In other leagues additional players may be placed on the field in any extra spots, other than one of the 9 regular baseball positions; filling any gaps with any extra players.

• For example, you can place an extra player between 1st and 2nd base and use 2 center field positions (right-center & left-center). You can also use 2 pitchers that are spread apart in the "Pitcher's Circle."

- When your team is on offense, you can have Coaches assisting and instructing in the following areas: One (1) coach helping the batter at the 'tee,' one (1) assistant coach at first base, and one (1) assistant coach at third base.

- When your team is on defense, you can use two (2) of your assistant coaches as defensive coaches in the outfield during play to assist the outfielders on where to throw the ball.

Manager and Coaches (Positions):

The Manager or any Coach may stand at the batting tee to adjust the batting tee; place the ball on the tee; and position the batter within the batter's box prior to each swing, if needed. The coach at the tee must remove the batting tee and the baseball bat after the ball is hit for obvious player safety reasons.

When on offense the first (1st) and third (3rd) base Coaches will umpire their respective bases. Managers or Coaches must stay at least three feet (3') behind the foul line when the ball is in play.

When on defense two (2) defensive Coaches will umpire the plays and calls made at second base. The Coach managing the batting tee will umpire the plays made at home plate and the fair or foul balls.

Keep It Moving-

Do your best to keep the game moving along smoothly and efficiently. Make all reasonable efforts to move the game along quickly. Teach your team to get on and off the field promptly by instructing them run on and off the field every time.

Now Go Have Fun!

CHAPTER TEN - Get the Parents Involved
Let the Parents Pick the Positions

For fun you can try this idea if you'd like later in the season. For one game you can let the parents, along with their child, decide which positions their son/daughter will play. Ahead of time give them a letter similar to the following one with a 'Position' sheet. This requires some thought and field coordinating on your part once you receive all of the requests, but you're already doing that by rotating the players through each position anyway. This will help with the parent who thinks their son/daughter should have been playing a certain position in their mind anyway. Plus, the kids get excited to make a 'coaching' decision.

Sample letter : (Feel free to type up a copy of this letter to use if you'd like).

Dear Parents,

I thought I would try something for one game just for added fun. You, the parents, can **pick the**

positions (*in 1 game*) that you would like   ς
your son/daughter play.

 We have (#) players on our team so probably need to do this over 3 or 4 games many parents and players will likely pick the positions. But for that one game you got to p. position.

 When it's your son/daughter's day, he/she most likely will be in the infield the entire game based on your choices, so the other players will probably be in the outfield most of the game. So keep this in mind when it is not your son/daughter's day to play your desired positions, as he/she may primarily be in the outfield during those few games.

 Fill out the 3 positions you would like to see your child play in during one game.

 I will try to organize these positions on paper and let you know which game your son/daughter will play your field positions.

Sound like fun? Great! Make sure you return your form to me as soon as possible.

> ❖ I have definitely been trying to rotate all of the players fairly throughout the positions and I hope everyone is happy. It is tough with so many kids to switch them around 100% fairly. Plus not every position is right for every child's ability for safety reasons.

Special note about Coaches pitching to the players:

Also, please keep in mind that we coaches are doing the best we can to pitch to the kids. It is very hard to consistently throw a ball straight over the plate at the exact height and speed for each player with both sidelines watching your every pitch. Believe me, we want every player to hit the balls we pitch to make us look good too.

Many of our players are learning to bat for the first time, so even good pitches get missed. Please bear with us, as none of us are Nolan Ryan or Cy Young.

YOU PICK THE POSITIONS (for 1 game)

1ST position:_____

2ND position:_____

3RD position:_____

4th position:_____
(in case of position overlap)

List of positions:

Infield:

1st base
2nd base
3rd base
Short Stop
Floater/Rover (between 1st & 2nd)
Pitcher
Catcher

Outfield:
Left, Center, Right
I'll try to accommodate your first 3 choices if possible.

The 4th choice gives me flexibility when trying to coordinate (#, the actual number of) players over 3 innings.

Closing Words To You, Coach

Well, remember, you got this Coach. You'll do great! Have fun, be fair and remember to smile a lot. Like I said in the section "Another Word on Demonstrating Good Sportsmanship" kids often remember their first coach for a long time, so give them good memories.

And one more thing; again as mentioned in Chapter Two, please don't be overly hard on your own little tee-ball player. Do not over-correct him/her or place unfair expectations on him/her. Your child does not have to be the best player just because he/she is the coach's kid. He/she will goof off and daydream just like the rest of your team. Remember, they are just kids and daydreaming and having fun is their main job as children.

And do not get caught up in not putting your child at first base or placing them first in the batting lineup in order to appear as though you are not "playing favorites". If you rotate every player fairly and decide to let your tee-ball player start as pitcher or first base, especially for the first game, then so be it. There are some privileges for accepting responsibility of managing an entire team after all. Just try not to do it every single game. So go out there and do your best!

Also, thank you very much for buying this book! We can all use a little guidance, a few reminders, and some helpful information that we either didn't already know or just didn't think about.

And finally, I'd just like to add, **PLAY BALL!**

Quick Review Workbook :

This workbook is meant as a Quick Review Reference Tool. It covers reminders for you. They include the initial team meeting, a list of delegated duties to others, practice and game responsibilities (before and after) and team parent duties. Just turn to this section for a quick reminder or to review important information.

First Team Meeting
• Welcome everyone and thank them for showing up at your first team meeting.
• Introduce yourself and include your experience.
• Parents Expectations of Coach:
(These are the things taught, coached and covered by you) :
> • Teach basic baseball skills.
> • Maintain a positive attitude.
> • Be on time for the practices and the games.
> • Demonstrate good sportsmanship at all times.

• The Coach's Expectations of Parents & Players:
(Things demonstrated by the parents) :
• Be <u>on time</u> for practices and *early* for games. Inform coach if they must leave early and if someone else will be picking up their child.
• Every player must let me know his or her parent is present before leaving.
• Positive Attitudes & Encouragement (for Both parents & players)

- Good Sportsmanship (Again for Both parents & players)
- Treat coach, assistant coaches, and team parent with _Respect_.

Equipment / Uniform:
- The league should provide a few batting helmets, baseball bats, balls and a batting tee, which has an adjustable height, flexible tube, and movable base.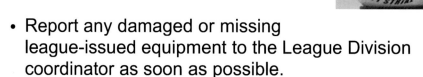
- Reduced factor Safety Balls - level one safety baseballs (sponge/rubber center) Shall be used.

- Report any damaged or missing league-issued equipment to the League Division coordinator as soon as possible.

- Make sure your players have the following:
Cleats (preferable)
Jerseys & caps (provided by the league). Jerseys must be tucked in.
Baseball pants
Glove
Bat
Batting helmet
Water bottles

Practices and Games:
- Practice twice a week for 1 hour (before the season starts).
  It goes to once a week for 1 hour (after the season starts).

- 2 Games played per week, @ 1 1/2 hours each: One midweek game & one every Saturday (Schedule released by the League).

Positions:
- Rotate positions initially every game.
- Assign players in the position that best suits them and the team as their skills and the season progresses.

3 Pitch Rule:
- Hitting the ball initially starts on the batting Tee.
- Actual pitching from the coach typically starts well before mid-season.

Typical League Rule: Batters are to receive <u>3 pitches only.</u> If they miss hitting the ball onto the field, then place the baseball onto the batting tee. (This rule applies even if the player repeatedly fouls off the ball.)

Additional Coaches:
- Request an Assistant Coach (or a few assistant coaches).
- Delegate duties to the assistant coaches to help run drills, to act as base coaches, etc.
- All coaches should check for dangerous debris on the field and in both dugouts (rocks, glass, etc.) before every practice and game.
- Assign an assistant coach to Player Safety for every practice and game. The Player Safety Coach keeps an eye on all of the players while you are busy instructing, demonstrating and

teaching. (Example: making sure a player is not walking up behind you or a batter who is about to swing the bat.) Safety violations or injuries should be reported immediately to the League Division Coordinator.

Request a Team Mom/Team Parent (TM/TP):
Team Mom/Team Parent responsibilities include —
• Collects money and orders the team banner
• Creates refreshment schedule for games
Refreshments: each parent is typically assigned a game day to bring light, healthy, refreshing snacks for each player along with a juice box or small store-bought water bottles.
• Collects candy fundraiser money to be turned in to the league,
• Orders trophies
• "End of season" team party
• Passes along information from the manager to the parents

Questions/Comments/Adjournment of the meeting:
• Answer questions.
• Meet the players and get their names and experience levels here too.
• Confirm league-provided contact information (email, phone numbers) with the parents of each member on your team.

Be Prepared (Practices and Games):
Always have a first aid kit with you and extra water bottles.

(For Practices) :
- Check for dangerous debris on the field and in both dugouts (rocks, glass, etc.)
- Write out a list of drills
- List of the players' names and assigned positions
- Warm up the players (Have players run the bases in the correct base order, calling out the bases as they step on them.)
- Bring extra water bottles

Field Rotation (Practices):
Each player hits off of the batting tee and runs through 1st base. The runner puts his batting helmet away, grabs his glove and goes to right field. The right fielder moves to his right over to center field, the center fielder moves over to left field and the left fielder goes to play 3rd base. The 3rd baseman moves to his left to short stop, the short stop moves to his left to 2nd base, 2nd baseman moves to his left to 1st base. The 1st baseman moves to the pitcher's spot and the pitcher is the next to bat. The movement is like a big "S" snake.

(Pre-Game) Home Team:
- Check for dangerous debris on the field and in both dugouts (rocks, glass, etc.)
- Chalk the Batter's boxes (on each side of home plate)
- Chalk the First and Third Baselines

- Chalk the Pitcher's circle around the Pitcher's mound/area
- Put bases into place (insert the pegs into base holes)
- Check the field for dangerous debris and in both dugouts (rocks, glass, etc.)

(For Games):
- Visiting team bats first.
- Make a list of the players' names and assigned positions for each inning of the game (typically 3 innings for tee-ball).
- Post a batting lineup in your dugout for the entire team to see. (List every position and then the players' names next to each position.)
  All players bat through the line-up each inning.
- Warm up the players (Have players run the bases in the correct base order calling out the bases as they step on them.)
- Always have on hand extra water bottles/snacks.

(Post-Game) Visiting Team:
- Check for dangerous debris on the field and in both dugouts (rocks, glass, etc.)
- Put bases away, (into league provided storage shed), if you have the last game of the day.

Field Position Names and Position Numbers:

POSITION	POSITION NUMBER
Pitcher	1
Catcher	2
1st Base	3
2nd Base	4
3rd Base	5
Short Stop	6
Left Fielder	7
Center Fielder	8
Right Fielder	9

Drill Ideas:

Take One

Throwing & Catching Drills

Shuffle, Shuffle, Dirt

Fielding Drill

Double Play at Home Plate

Glossary of Terms

Ball: An errant pitch which does not enter the strike zone and is not swung at by the batter.

Base (bag): The padded targets placed into the ground at the 3 corners of the baseball diamond (not including the fourth corner, which is home plate).
The bases must be touched (from 1st, 2nd, 3rd to Home Plate) by each runner in order to score a run.

Batter: The offensive player who is currently standing in the batter's box.

Batter's Box: One of 2 chalked areas next to home plate where the batter stands during his time at bat. (The batter stands either facing right or left of the catcher.)

Bottom (of the inning): The second half of any inning.

Bunt: A legally batted ball, that is intentionally not hit hard with the bat, but rather tapped onto the infield.

Catch: The act of any fielder receiving or getting secure possession of the baseball into his hand or glove while the ball is in flight and maintaining possession it.

Catcher: The defensive player position that is positioned directly behind home plate and the batter.

Defense: The players currently in their positions on the playing field.

Double (hit): (Not used in Tee-Ball, **for Info Only**) -
A play in which the batter hits the ball and runs uninterrupted to second base before stopping.

Double Play: A defensive play in which two offensive players are put out as a result of one continuous action. (For example, A 2nd baseman catches a ball that was hit into the air, and then throws it to the first baseman before the runner who has left 1st base can return to it. Thus resulting in a double play).

Dugout: The seating area for the players that are not currently on the playing field, at bat or next to bat (standing in the on deck area).

Fair Ball: A batted baseball that touches the playing field within or on the chalked (designated) fair territory lines. If it touches this area before striking 1st or 3rd base and then going into foul territory, it is still deemed fair and playable. If it travels past 1st or 3rd base, touches the field or a defensive player, and then goes into foul territory it is still deemed fair and playable.

Fair Territory: All parts of the chalked (designated) playing field. This includes the areas within and including the first base and third base lines, straight back into the outfield, and from home plate to the farthest playing field fence (or wall).

Fielder: Any one of the 9 defensive players, including the pitcher, catcher, first baseman, second baseman, third baseman, shortstop, left fielder, center fielder and right fielder.

Fielder's Choice: The act of a fielder who handles a fair, batted ground ball and, instead of throwing to first base to put out the batter/runner, throws to another base in an attempt to put out a preceding runner.

Fielding: The act of catching or retrieving a hit or thrown baseball on the field of play. It can include even catching the ball in the air for an "out" even in fielded in foul territory.

Field Rotation: Rotating players through the different field positions to give them experience in each position and to make them well-rounded baseball players.

Floater (Field position) : See also "Rover"
An additional player(s) placed on the field in any extra spot(s), other than one of the 9 regular baseball positions; filling any gaps with any extra players.

For example, you can place an extra player between 1st and 2nd base and use 2 center field positions (right-center & left-center). You can also use 2 pitchers that are spread apart in the "Pitcher's Circle."

Fly Ball: A ball which goes high into the air when batted.

Fly Out : An out resulting in a player on the field catching and maintaining possession of a hit ball before it touches the ground.

Force Out : When a player is *"forced"* to run to the next base because the batter hits a fair ball and advances to first base after getting the hit.

Force Play: A play in which a runner loses his right to occupy a base when the current batter becomes a runner and runs to that same base.

Foul Ball: A baseball that is batted, but does not stay within the marked (chalked) boundaries of fair territory. Example: a batted baseball that lands in foul territory, such as between home plate and before either first base or third base, or touches out of bounds once past either first or third base.

Foul Territory: The areas that are not within the marked boundaries of fair territory. Example: outside of the marked (chalked) first and third base lines extending to the outfield fence or wall.

Ground Ball: A batted baseball which rolls along the ground anywhere within fair territory.

Ground Rule Double: When a hit baseball bounces on the playing field and then over the fence or wall within fair territory it is counted as a ground rule double and the batter may only advance to second base.

Home Plate: The white, 5-sided plate over which an offensive player bats in front of the catcher. The batter after getting a hit must return to home plate after touching all three bases in order to score a run.

Home Run: A play in which the batter either hits the ball over the outfield fence (or wall), or is able to run around all three bases and return to home plate without stopping.

Home Team: The team on whose field the game is played is considered the home team. If both teams play on the same field then the home team shall be designated by the league during the game scheduling.

Infield: The front half or diamond-shaped area of the playing field, which is bordered by the 3 bases and home plate.

Infielder: A player who is assigned a position within the infield.

Inning: That portion of the game in which both teams alternate on offense and defense and in which each team has the offense until they get three outs and then switch places with their opponent until they get three outs, thereby ending the inning for both teams. Therefore each team's completed time at bat is half of one inning.

Line Drive: A ball that is hit but does not touch the ground. It goes straight from the bat to either a defensive player, up the field, or up the chalked lines in fair territory.

Offense: The team currently at bat until they get 3 outs. Then they switch places with the opposing players on the field and become defense.

Out: When a batter hits a ball that is caught in mid air, or swings and misses the ball to gain 3 strikes, or a runner is tagged with the ball by a defensive layer. Each team is at bat until they get 3 outs.

Outfield: The area that extends beyond the front half or diamond-shaped area of the playing field, which is bordered by the marked (chalked) first and third baselines.

The outfield has 3 players on it, (the LF, CF, RF), except for tee-ball which may have more.

Outfielder: A player who is assigned a position within the outfield.

Pitch: A ball that is thrown by the pitcher to the batter and towards the catcher's mitt.

Pitcher: The player assigned to pitch the ball to the batter and towards the catcher's mitt.

Pitcher's Circle: The chalked circle around the pitcher's mound and pitcher's rubber plate. The pitcher must stand in this designated area.

Pop Fly Ball: A ball that is hit directly into the air, usually in a high arching path.

Rover (Field position):   see also "Floater"

An additional player(s) placed on the field in any extra spot(s), other than one of the 9 regular baseball positions; filling any gaps with any extra players.

For example, you can place an extra player between 1st and 2nd base and use 2 center field positions (right-center & left-center). You can also use 2 pitchers that are spread apart in the "Pitcher's Circle."

Run: A run is a score made by any offensive player who has successfully rounded the 3 bases and returned to home plate.

Runner: After an offensive player hits the baseball in or over fair territory he becomes a runner. He then advances toward and touches each base before stopping on any base or successfully returning to home plate.

Safe: A runner is deemed safe is he successfully runs to any base before being tagged or forced out, and is therefore is entitled to stop and occupy that base.

Single: A play in which the batter hits the ball and runs safely to first base.

Strike: (Not used in Tee-Ball, **for Info Only**) - When a baseball is pitched to the batter and one of the following examples occurs:

1 The batter swings the bat at the ball, but misses;
2 The ball passes through the strike zone without being hit by the batter;
3 The batter hits the ball into foul territory and when he has less than two strikes already;
4 The ball touches the batter as he swings and makes contact with the baseball within the strike zone;
5 After the batter hits the ball it travels directly from the bat into the catcher's mitt and is caught by the catcher (considered a foul tip).

Strike Zone: Not used in Tee-Ball.

Tag: The action of a fielder touching a base with his body while holding the ball, or touching a runner with the ball, or with his hand or glove while holding the baseball.

Throw: The act of propelling the ball toward a teammate so that they may receive (catch) the baseball. Including an underhand throw from the player with the baseball. Note: A pitch is not considered a throw.

Top (of the Inning): The first half of any inning.

Triple (hit): (Not used in Tee-Ball, **for Info Only**) - A play in which the batter runs uninterrupted from first to third base without stopping after hitting the baseball.

Triple Play: (Not used in Tee-Ball, **for Info Only**) - A defensive play in which three separate offensive players are put "out" during one continuous action.

Umpire: Not used in Tee-Ball.

Index of Terms:

Double Play: (Not used in Tee-Ball, **for Info Only**) -
A defensive play in which two offensive players are put out as a result of one continuous action. (For example, A 2nd baseman catches a ball that was hit into the air, and then throws it to the first baseman before the runner who has left 1st base can return to it. Thus resulting in a double play).

Fair Ball: A batted baseball that touches the playing field within or on the chalked (designated) fair territory lines. If it touches this area before striking 1st or 3rd base and then going into foul territory, it is still deemed fair and playable. If it travels past 1st or 3rd base, touches the field or a defensive player, and then goes into foul territory it is still deemed fair and playable.

Fielding: The act of catching or retrieving a hit or thrown baseball on the field of play. It can include even catching the ball in the air for an "out" even in fielded in foul territory.

Field Rotation: Rotating players through the different field positions to give them experience in each position and to make them well-rounded baseball players.

Foul Ball: A baseball that is batted, but does not stay within the marked (chalked) boundaries of fair territory.
Example: a batted baseball that lands in foul territory, such as between home plate and before either first base or third base, or touches out of bounds once past either first or third base.

Floater (Field position) : See also "Rover"
An additional player(s) placed on the field in any extra spot(s), other than one of the 9 regular baseball positions, filling any gaps with any extra players.
For example, you can place an extra player between 1st and 2nd base and use 2 center field positions (right-center & left-center). You can also use 2 pitchers that are spread apart in the "Pitcher's Circle."

Fly Out: An out resulting in a player on the field catching and maintaining possession of a hit ball before it touches the ground.

Force Out: When a player is "*forced*" to run to the next base because the batter hits a fair ball and advances to first base after getting the hit.

Line Drive: A ball that is hit but does not touch the ground. Straight from the bat to either a defensive player, up the field or up the fair territory chalked lines.

Pitcher's Circle: The chalked circle around the pitcher's mound and pitcher's rubber plate. The pitcher must stand in this designated area.

Pop Fly Ball: A ball that is hit directly into the air, usually in a high arch.

Rover (Field position):   see also "Floater"
An additional player(s) placed on the field in any extra spot(s), other than one of the 9 regular baseball positions; filling any gaps with any extra players.

For example, you can place an extra player between 1st and 2nd base and use 2 center field positions (right-center & left-center). You can also use 2 pitchers that are spread apart in the "Pitcher's Circle."

Tag or Tags (any runner, base or home plate): To step on (or actually touch with any body part such as a hand or foot) any base or home plate while in possession of the ball before the runner touches that same base or home plate with any part of his body.
Also completed by a defensive player who touches a runner with the ball itself, or with his glove while holding the ball inside of the glove.

Team Mom/Team Parent: A helper who is a parent of one of the players, who will assist by arranging a game refreshment schedule, collecting any fundraising money, ordering a team-name banner, organizing end of year team party, passes along information from the manager to the parents, etc.

ABOUT THE AUTHOR

Douglas P. Kalbaugh is a husband to a beautiful, loving wife, and a father to
3 incredible sons. Doug has coached youth sports, including baseball and soccer, for over 10 years. He was formerly a Patrol Police Officer for almost 15 years, but wrote this guide while he was a mechanical draftsman working for a medical company.